Joan of Arc

A Cherrytree Book

Designed and produced by
A S Publishing

First published 1989
by Cherrytree Press Ltd
a subsidiary of
The Chivers Company Ltd
Windsor Bridge Road
Bath, Avon BA2 3AX

Copyright © Cherrytree Press Ltd 1989

British Library Cataloguing in Publication Data

Williams, Brian,
   Joan of Arc.
   1. France. Joan of Arc, Saint, 1412-1431
   I. Title II. Series
   944'.026'0924

ISBN 0-7451-5031-4

Printed in Hong Kong by Colorcraft Ltd

CHILDREN OF HISTORY

Joan of Arc

By Brian Williams · *Illustrated by* Gwen Green

CHERRYTREE BOOKS

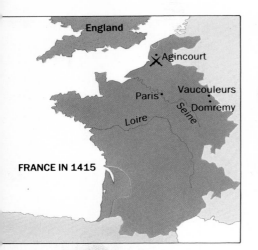

England

Agincourt

Vaucouleurs

Paris

Domremy

Seine

Loire

FRANCE IN 1415

HUNDRED YEARS'
WAR (1337-1453)
This struggle raged
intermittently between
England and France for
more than a century. Five
French kings had fought
five English kings for
control of France. The
Battle of Agincourt was
fought on 25 October
1415. The English army
was smaller than the
French, and supposedly
weak after marching for 17
days. The proud French
knights jostled for places in
the front rank. Crowded
together, their horses
became bogged down in
muddy ground and the
knights struggled
helplessly beneath a hail of
English arrows.

Born in a Troubled France

In the year 1412, a baby girl was born in the village of
Domrémy in France. She was the daughter of Jacques and
Isabelle d'Arc, the ploughman and his wife. They named
their daughter Jeanne – Jeanne d'Arc. We know her as Joan
of Arc, the brave girl who led the French army to victory
over the English and bravely faced the cruel death they
inflicted on her.

When Joan was born, France had been at war for a long
time – at war with England and with itself. The country was
divided. The army of Henry V, King of England (and of
France, as he claimed), held much of the north. The
powerful Duke of Burgundy, John the Fearless, was a king
in all but name. Burgundy joined forces with the English to
try to overthrow the feeble French monarch – Charles VI,
head of the royal house of Valois and quite mad.

The War Comes Close

So far the war had hardly affected Joan's family. Domrémy
was a village of no importance. Few of the villagers knew
much about the world beyond their winding River Meuse
and its peaceful meadows. Only bad news sped across
country. Little Joan heard but could not have understood
the news that shocked the villagers in October 1415. There
had been a battle at a place called Agincourt, and the
French had lost 10,000 men.

Joan's parents did not know where Agincourt was, but
they were afraid. They said prayers in church for the safety
of France and for themselves. The countryside would not
be safe with soldiers and brigands about. There was nothing
they could do but simply pray for peace.

Joan was only three when
the villagers of Domrémy
heard the news of France's
defeat at the battle of Agincourt.

A Medieval Family

Joan's family was hard-working and well respected in Domrémy. The villagers lived by farming. They tilled the strips of land on either side of the river and kept cattle, pigs, sheep and geese. The soil was rich, and in a good year there was food for everyone. Winter was the hardest time, when people 'tightened their belts' and made do with salted meat and fish.

The France England hoped to rule was still rich, despite years of war. Throughout the land, people worked to the rhythm of the seasons. Joan knew them well. January and

Jacques d'Arc worked with the other men in the fields from dawn to dusk. Joan liked to bring him his midday meal. She kept a watchful eye on the geese, which insisted on following her.

February were too wet and cold to do much work in the fields, but in March the farming year began. Her father would yoke his oxen and drive them to the fields to begin the spring ploughing. As the new crops were sown, the lord de Baudricourt would ride out from his castle to inspect the royal lands, to hawk and to hunt in the forests. June and July were the months of haymaking and harvest. In September grapes were gathered from the vines, ready to be made into wine. In November, the pigs would be driven to the forest to root for acorns and the villagers would gather wood for their fires. Then, in a good year, there would be feasting, songs and winter's tales.

FOOD FOR THE RICH
The village priest gave the children lessons in religion and amused them with stories about life in the great hall of Robert de Baudricourt. He told them mouth-watering tales of the fine dishes on the lord's table: crayfish, soft bread, wine, huge eel pies, tender beans cooked in milk and enormous fruit tarts.

In winter, with everyone crowded around the fire and the windows shuttered, the house was quite snug. Joan worked at her mending while her brothers played fivestones with knucklebones.

At Home

Joan and her family lived in a small house, with a slate roof and a mud floor. The oxen were kept in a stall next door, so the children could hear the animals moving about in the straw. Joan had three brothers. They told Joan that they prayed to become famous soldiers with fine clothes and horses. Joan laughed at them (though she thought they ought to pray for better things). Joan's mother Isabelle was a devout Christian. She taught the children prayers and hymns and made sure that the whole family went to church.

After the death of her sister Catherine, Joan was the only girl. She helped her mother in the home, fetching water, cooking, mending, and minding her brothers. Joan did not go to school, and never learnt to read or write. She rose from her bed at sunrise and worked until sunset; candles were too expensive for ordinary folk.

Visiting the Fairy Tree

The best time of the year was early summer when the leaves in the forest were freshly green, and the days were getting longer. The village children would go into the forest to play. Among the ancient oak trees, there was one huge, low-branching beech. This was a fairy tree (so the younger children believed), sacred to woodland sprites older than the forest itself.

For generations, children from Domrémy had visited this spot to hang garlands of flowers from the boughs of the fairy tree. The younger ones danced around it, while the others tried to frighten one another with tales of fairies, elves and Merlin the magician. Joan enjoyed her visits to the tree, though she did not believe in fairies or anything magical. As she grew older, she was happier going to church.

Ruin and Pestilence

THE PLAGUE
The outbreak of plague in 1418 was small compared to the one that had ravaged Europe seventy years earlier. Known as the Black Death, it had killed one in three Europeans. The disease, which is spread by rats, is easily treated with antibiotics and is rare today. But medieval medicine could do little to check such epidemics, or treat the victims.

While Joan was growing up, the French monarchy was in trouble. The mad king's eldest son Louis had died in 1415. When his second son Jean died in 1416, the youngest son Charles became Dauphin (heir to the throne). A youth of little promise, Charles was in the care of the powerful Constable of France, Bernard d'Armagnac. In June 1418, Armagnac and thousands of his followers were massacred in Paris by Burgundians. At 15, Charles's cause seemed hopeless – he would never be king.

Patiently, Henry of England waited for France to fall into his grip. The year 1418 was a terrible one for the French. People died in their thousands as the English army laid siege to the city of Rouen. There was famine throughout the

land, for the fields were unploughed, and no crops gathered in. The Bishop of Lisieux wrote sadly in his journal that France was: 'uncultivated, abandoned, overgrown with brushwood and brambles'.

Watching at the Gate

To add to these miseries came a new horror. There was an outbreak of plague in Paris. Terrified townsfolk fled into the countryside to escape the deadly disease. Every village posted watchmen to scan the roads and keep out strangers. Everyone feared the plague. In Domrémy the village children watched from a safe distance as bedraggled refugees pleaded with the villagers. 'This is all the food we can spare' Joan heard her father explain. 'Wolves attack what few sheep we have left. Go, with our prayers.'

The people fleeing from the plague looked exhausted. But the villagers dared not allow them to stay. Joan and her brothers hid in the bushes and looked on as the village watchmen turned away the travellers. She felt great pity for the refugees.

Fighting One Another

Joan never forgot the faces of the travellers, as they went wearily on their way. Where could they hope to find refuge? She prayed each night for peace and an end to France's torment. But for Domrémy things were getting worse.

It was easy for the villagers to repel unarmed refugees weakened by illness and hunger. It was less easy for them to fend off marauding soldiers – English, French and Burgundian alike – who stole their cattle and killed their sheep and pigs. The villagers were grateful for the protection of the nearby castle of Bourlemont, and for help given to them by Robert de Baudricourt, the governor of the town of Vaucouleurs.

Civil Strife

Life was not peaceful even among the children. The civil war in France divided neighbouring villages. Domrémy had always been on the side of Charles the Dauphin. The villagers of Maxey, a mile or so away, were supporters of the Duke of Burgundy.

Rivalry between the two villages was strong, and extended to the children. The two sides fought, sometimes violently. Armed with sticks and stones, the Domrémy children went to war with Maxey to teach the Burgundians a lesson.

Both sides returned from these battles bruised and bloodied. Joan was as fervent as anyone in supporting the Dauphin's cause, but she would not join in the brawls. She hated to see the French fighting one another, whether they were children or soldiers. If people had to fight, they should fight together against the English, in support of the Dauphin who was the rightful heir to France.

When the Domrémy boys battled with their Maxey rivals, Joan helped bandage the wounds caused by cudgels and flying stones, but she would have preferred them not to fight at all.

The Throne of France for England?

In 1420, France seemed almost within England's grasp. First, the Duke of Burgundy had been assassinated while seeking to make peace with the Dauphin. Burgundy's successor Philip blamed the Dauphin for the murder and threw in his lot with the English. Then King Charles VI (now too ill to rule) agreed that Henry of England, and not the Dauphin, should have the crown of France on his death. Henry married the King's daughter Catherine and waited to claim the crown of France.

Confusion and Villainy

The civil war in France made good government impossible. It seemed that the situation could not be worse, but in 1422, on the verge of his triumph, Henry V of England died of dysentery. His infant son Henry VI was left in the care of the Duke of Bedford. Poor mad Charles VI of France was also dead. Now no one knew who would be king.

In the confusion, local barons and fortune hunters seized any chance to increase their power and wealth. The villages suffered unless they stood their ground, and Domrémy was no exception. Besides paying lawful taxes, the villagers were at the mercy of bullies and bandits.

Jacques d'Arc Takes a Stand

Joan watched with pride as her father stood up to one such bully. A soldier named Robert de Saarbruck marched into Domrémy and demanded payment from every family in return for his 'protection'. Jacques d'Arc was now village dean. It fell to him to confront de Saarbruck.

Resolutely, Joan's father refused to quail as de Saarbruck blustered and threatened. 'We are poor people,' he explained quietly. 'We pay what is due to the Dauphin. We need pay no more, and he will protect us.' The other villagers gathered behind the defiant ploughman. The bogus tax collectors slunk away to seek easier pickings.

Joan's father was a peace-loving man but he would not give in to threats. He knew what taxes the villagers had to pay, and he would pay no more – least of all to a local bully.

15

Miraculous Visions

Until she was 13, Joan's life was no different from that of any other village girl. She could spin and sew and cook, and (though he said nothing as yet) her father already had a young man in mind to become her husband. But everything changed one summer's day. And ever since, people have wondered exactly what it was that happened to Joan.

On this sunny morning, she was minding the sheep, and enjoying the brightness of the flowers close to the church, when it seemed that a great stillness closed about her. A radiance, brighter than the sun, dazzled her eyes and she heard a voice. It spoke to her, as a friend. 'Be a virtuous and good girl and go to church frequently,' the voice told her. And then the light vanished.

The Saints' Message

Not long afterwards, Joan had another, even more startling, experience. Three saints – she said they were St Michael, St Catherine and St Margaret – appeared before her. They told her that she must one day leave home and go to the aid of the King of France, in order to return him to his rightful throne. What could it all mean?

Joan was to hear her voices many more times thereafter, and they changed her life. Never again could she be just another village girl. From now on she was the 'mystic maid' of Domrémy, and the message her saints gave her was discussed far and wide.

Not surprisingly, Joan's parents were perplexed. Isabelle d'Arc believed her daughter was sincere. But how could a peasant girl possibly do what the saints asked? Jacques d'Arc took a more down-to-earth view: when Joan was married there would be an end to voices and visions.

JOAN'S SAINTS
The three saints whom Joan saw, and who spoke to her, were (left to right) St Catherine of Alexandria, St Michael the Archangel and St Margaret of Antioch. It was through these heavenly messengers, she said, that she received God's commands.

Joan fell to her knees in wonder when she heard her 'voices'. Her visions were intense religious experiences and inspired the young girl with the belief that she had a divine mission to save France.

16

SOUND OF BELLS
Ringing bells alerted the villagers whenever trouble threatened. Church bells were also rung to mark saints' days, baptisms of children, and funerals. People told the time by the regular peal of the angelus bell (for morning, noon and sunset prayers). Joan loved to hear the bells, and always remembered their sound as one special to her childhood.

Escape by Night

In 1428, the war came to Joan's own village. The English and their Burgundian allies planned to attack the Dauphin's last bastions and so end the war. The governor of the province of Champagne (who supported Burgundy) sent soldiers to raid the pro-Dauphin territory where Joan lived. One night, enemy soldiers attacked Domrémy.

Flight to the Castle
Joan was roused from her bed by the clamour of the alarm bell. The watchmen were shouting, the dogs were barking, and there were sounds of confusion everywhere. Dashing

18

outside, Joan was horrified to see flames leaping into the night sky. The church was on fire. So was the great barn. People were running from their homes in panic; figures loomed out of the shadows but in the darkness it was impossible to tell friend from foe.

Joan's brothers grabbed clubs and pitchforks to do battle with the Burgundians. Their father shouted to everyone to run to the river. They must cross to the island and take shelter inside the castle. At the water's edge Joan helped the little children scramble into a boat. She told them not to be scared, for no Burgundians would dare attack the castle. The cowardly raiders had done their night's work and would not stay to fight.

As the men did their best to beat off the Burgundian raiders, Joan helped the younger children to safety. They jumped into a boat, and she pushed it out into the river. Once inside the stone walls of the castle, they would be safe.

19

Joan Leaves Home

The church was repaired, the barn rebuilt. But there was no peace in the land, and no rest for Joan. She continued to hear her voices; always their message was the same. Her father strove to persuade her to forget all about 'voices' and marry the husband he had chosen for her. But Joan was unshakeable. She could not marry. She insisted that she must obey her voices. She must go to the Dauphin's aid. He had fled south across the River Loire to the stronghold of Chinon. As a first step Joan must persuade Robert de Baudricourt to help her on her mission.

She found an ally in a relative, Durand Laxart, who agreed to take Joan to Vaucouleurs and obtained permission for her to see the governor. Joan knew her father would be angry, so she left home without permission. Durand lent her an old horse for the journey.

This Girl May be a Witch

De Baudricourt was as baffled as Jacques d'Arc. His instinct was to send Joan home, with a scolding. But there was something about her; she spoke boldly, without fear. 'France belongs not to the Dauphin alone, but to God,' she declared, and begged him to help her.

The nobleman sought the advice of his priest. Might not this girl be a witch? The priest visited Joan at her lodgings. Sprinkling holy water over himself, in case Joan was possessed by the devil, he confronted her and demanded that any evil spirits depart from her. Joan knelt before him, to ask his blessing, and the priest was convinced.

'My Lord, she is no witch,' he reported. De Baudricourt pondered what to do. Joan was now a celebrity. The townsfolk had given her food, clothing, even a better horse. Clearly, there was something about her. He sent a message to the Dauphin, telling Charles that the miraculous maid, *La Pucelle* (the virgin), was on her way.

Joan's First Followers

Two battle-hardened knights, Jean de Metz and Bertrand de Poulengy, had also talked with Joan. Their first reaction of scorn and amusement had turned to admiration and hope. 'I would rather stay with my mother and spin,' Joan said, 'yet I must go, for it is the Lord's will.' The two soldiers vowed to go with Joan, to protect and escort her on the next dangerous stage of her mission.

Her parents arrived, pleading with her to come home. But Joan was adamant. She must go to the Dauphin.

In medieval times, people believed in witches, who were thought to be the devil's helpers. Some people feared Joan because of her voices, but the priest's blessing reassured de Baudricourt that Joan was not a witch.

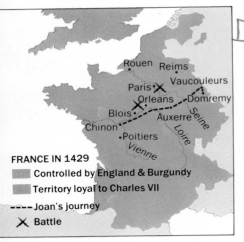

FRANCE IN 1429
- ■ Controlled by England & Burgundy
- ■ Territory loyal to Charles VII
- ---- Joan's journey
- ✕ Battle

Joan's mission took her first from Vaucouleurs to Chinon: then to Poitiers before her triumph at Orléans. At Reims the Dauphin was crowned, and finally at Rouen Joan's brief life came to an end.

A Dangerous Ride

Joan's mission to save France began on 13 February 1429. Her family watched her go, fearful of what lay in store. Joan herself had no fears. But, for the journey to Chinon, 11 days' ride away, she had been persuaded to change her clothes. The journey lay through territory where there was every chance of ambush. Joan would be safer dressed as a man.

So Joan's hair was cropped short, like a boy's. Instead of her old red dress, she now wore a man's shirt, breeches and doublet; and she had to bear the good-natured jokes of her companions. With her rode Jean de Metz and Bertrand de Poulengy, and four other men at arms. Joan soon got used to the strangeness of wearing men's clothes, but the first day's ride left her sore and stiff.

The Sword in the Chapel

At Joan's request, they stopped to pray at the chapel of St Catherine de Fierbois. St Catherine was the patron saint of runaway captives and prisoners of war, and the chapel was hung with chains and fetters. Joan knew this was a special place. Some days later, after they had reached Chinon, Joan told her friends that a sword lay hidden behind the altar. They found it, just as she said: the blade was rusty, but in Joan's hand the rust fell away to reveal the brilliance of bright steel. It was this sword that she would carry into battle for France.

How distant Domrémy now seemed, with its sheep and quiet meadows. Fearing for their lives, the seven rode mostly by night, skirting enemy watchfires. Finally, they reached the River Vienne, and saw before them the huge fortress of Chinon. Inside the three encircling walls of the castle was the Dauphin.

The journey to Chinon took Joan and her escort through enemy-held territory. They crossed the River Loire at Gien and rode on until they approached the huge castle which sheltered the Dauphin.

Joan Greets her Dauphin

Only within Chinon Castle's massive stone walls did Charles feel safe from his enemies. But who was this girl from Domrémy: friend or foe? His advisers told him not to listen to the 'voices' of a mere peasant girl. She must be mad, or worse, an agent of the devil. At best, she was yet another fraud, a false prophet out to cheat the gullible Dauphin. Charles was weary of listening to the arguments.

Now that Joan was in Chinon, waiting for an audience, Charles resolved to see her. Still fearful of being tricked, he agreed to a trial of Joan's 'powers'.

'I am Joan the Maid'

Charles changed his clothes, dressing like one of his knights, and mingled with the other courtiers as they gathered in the great hall. Around him were his remaining followers and hangers-on. Their finery looked shabby and patched, after years of war and defeat.

In walked Joan, followed by her escort. She halted a moment, looked about the throng of faces, and then strode purposefully forward. She pushed through the knights, and her gaze fell directly on Charles. Kneeling at his feet, she declared for all to hear: 'Gentle Dauphin, I am Joan the Maid; through me you will be crowned King at Reims.'

Joan had been in Chinon two days before the Dauphin agreed to see her. She was not taken in by his ruse, and immediately picked him out from among his courtiers, even though she had never even seen a picture of him.

Victory at Orléans

Charles was ready to grasp any straw to help secure his crown. He sent Joan to Poitiers, to be questioned by learned priests of the university, and was reassured when they found no evil in her. Joan told him her plan: it was simple, but astounding. She would raise the siege of Orléans. First, she dictated a letter to the English, calling on them to abandon their war and return home.

Joan the Warrior

Joan rode out from Chinon fully armed and mounted on a warhorse. She was attended by a squire and two pages, and among her escort were her brothers Jean and Pierre. Above

Joan was in the thick of the fighting at Orléans (left). She urged on her men as they stormed the English defences at Les Tourelles.

While scaling an assault ladder she was wounded, hit in the shoulder by an arrow. Despite the injury, she was quickly back in the battle, to lead the French to victory.

her floated a great white banner made at her order; it bore gold fleurs de lys (the flowers of France) and images of Jesus and the archangels Michael and Gabriel.

Joan and her relief column reached the great city of Orléans which was encircled by English forts. Her arrival seemed to have a miraculous effect on the French troops and their weary commanders. With new hope, the French attacked the main English strongpoint, at the fort of Les Tourelles. Joan would not use her sword but she braved every danger and was wounded. Even then she urged on her soldiers. 'Take my banner,' she commanded, 'and there will be no more difficulty.'

As the French rushed forward, bearing Joan's banner, the English defenders broke and retreated, leaving the city to the young girl and her rejoicing soldiers.

27

The royal crown was placed on Charles's head and he was anointed with holy oil by the Archbishop of Reims. Now he was France's rightful king. Joan had made this triumph possible.

The Crowning Glory

Joan knew that one victory was not enough. To secure his throne, Charles must be crowned at Reims. Yet still he dithered, forever plotting some new scheme.

The battle-weary captains took Joan to their hearts. They even stopped swearing at her demand and regularly went to church. In a few weeks, her inspiration had turned the tide. The English faltered, while Frenchmen flocked to join the Dauphin's army.

On 17 July 1429, the coronation of Charles VII took place in Reims Cathedral. Joan's parents were honoured guests at the ceremony. She herself, weeping tears of joy, stood close to Charles throughout, her banner beside her. Her king was crowned, the will of God accomplished.

Defeat and Disappointment

After triumph came disappointment, and then disaster, as the war continued. Joan's first defeat was in September when the French failed to capture Paris from the Burgundians. Because the attack was made on a feastday of the Virgin Mary, some people blamed Joan for fighting on a holy day. In fact, she had tried to prevent the attack.

Joan campaigned through the winter, still confident of final victory. Her brothers had been ennobled by the king (and now had fine horses and clothes), but she herself refused all honours and titles. The English (with Burgundian help) still hoped to make their boy-king Henry VI ruler of France; if they could get their hands on 'Joan the witch', they might yet depose Charles. Charles, for his part, conspired to bribe the Burgundians over to his side.

Joan is Captured

On 23 May 1430, Joan fell into her enemies' grasp. She was leading an expedition to the town of Compiègne which was under attack by Burgundians. While on a sortie outside the walls, she was unhorsed and taken prisoner.

Her captor was Jean de Ligny, whose wife treated Joan kindly while the English and Burgundians bargained for her life. Charles made no effort to pay a ransom for Joan's release. Instead the Burgundians accepted English gold and Joan was handed over to Pierre Cauchon, Bishop of Beauvais. Cauchon was in the pay of the English. He hated and feared Joan; he intended to see her tried for heresy – as a witch and enemy of the Church.

A few months after the coronation, Joan was a captive. After she tried to escape, she was kept under close guard and in chains. Her captors even refused to allow her to attend church.

Saint and Martyr

Joan's trial took place in Rouen. The written records show how well she spoke in her defence, even when sick and wretched after months chained in a dark prison cell.

She was accused of witchcraft, for which the punishment might be death. Her accusers gave her no rest, egged on by the English who were determined that Joan should not go free. She promised to obey the Church, and to give up her men's clothes, but she would not deny that her voices came from God.

There was no rescue, no escape. On 30 May 1431, Joan was burned at the stake in the market place of Rouen. From the ashes of the fire arose a spirit to unite France, the spirit of Saint Joan that lives on to this day.

An English soldier handed a small wooden cross to Joan as the fire took hold. A French priest held up another before her. Afterwards her enemies ordered her ashes to be scattered in the river so that no trace of her should remain.

Important Events in the Life of Joan of Arc and After

1412 Joan is born at Domrémy.
1413 Henry V becomes King of England.
1415 Battle of Agincourt (25 October).
1419 John the Fearless, Duke of Burgundy, is murdered.
1420 Charles VI of France agrees that Henry V of England shall be the next King of France.
1422 Deaths of both Charles VI of France and Henry V of England.
1425 Joan first hears her voices.
1428 Joan leaves home for the first time, to travel to Vaucouleurs.
1429 February: Joan rides to Chinon to see the Dauphin.
1429 May: Joan leads the French to victory at Orléans.
1429 July: The Dauphin is crowned Charles VII of France.
1429 September: Joan fails to capture Paris from the Burgundians.
1430 Joan is captured at Compiègne.

1431 January: Joan is put on trial at Rouen.
1431 24 May: Joan agrees to obey the Church and put on women's clothes again.
1431 30 May: After withdrawing her 'confession', Joan is put to death.

After Joan's Death

1431 December: Henry VI of England is crowned King of France in Paris, but the English have lost the war.
1437 Charles VII takes Paris.
1453 End of the Hundred Years' War between England and France.
1456 The Pope declares Joan innocent of any crime against the Church.
1461 Death of Charles VII.
1920 Joan is canonized, as Saint Joan. In France 24 June is a national holiday in her honour.

Index

Agincourt 4, 5
Arc, Catherine, d' 9
Arc, Isabelle d' 4, 9, 16, 21, 28
Arc, Jacques d' 4, 6, 7, 11, 15, 16,
 19-21, 28
Arc, Jean d' 26
Arc, Jeanne d' See Joan of Arc
Arc, Pierre d' 26
Armagnac, Bernard d' 10, 12
Armagnacs 12
Auxerre 22 (map)

Banner, Joan's 27, 29
Baudricourt, Robert de 7, 12, 20,
 21
Bedford, Duke of 14
Blois 22 (map)
Bourlemont, Castle of 12
Burgundians 10, 12, 18, 19, 29, 31
Burgundy, John, Duke of 4, 12,
 13, 31
Burgundy, Philip, Duke of 13
Burgundy, territory of 22 (map)

Catherine de Fierbois, St 22
Catherine of Alexandria, St 16
Cauchon, Pierre 29
Charles VI 4, 10, 13, 14, 31
Charles VII 28, 29, 31 See also
 Dauphin
Chinon 20, 22-26, 31
Compiègne 29, 31
Coronation 28

Dauphin 10, 12, 13, 15, 18, 20-26,
 31 See also Charles VII
Domrémy 4, 5, 6, 9, 11-16, 18, 22,
 24, 31

England 4, 6, 13, 22, 31
English 4, 10, 12, 13, 18, 26-31

Fairy tree 9
Farming 6, 7
France 4-6, 10-16, 22, 27-31
French 4, 10, 12, 26-29, 31

Gabriel, Archangel 27

Henry V 4, 10, 13, 14, 31
Henry VI 14, 29, 31
Hundred Years' War 4, 31

Jeanne d'Arc See Joan of Arc
Jesus 27
Joan of Arc
 birth of 4; family of 4, 6-9; early
 life of 4-15; home of 8, 9; visits
 fairy tree 9; pities plague
 refugees 11; disapproves of civil
 war 12; hears voices and sees
 visions 16; husband planned for
 16; saves children from fire 18,
 19; leaves home 20; gains
 support for mission 21; journey
 to Chinon 22; wears men's
 clothes 22; discovers sword 22;
 meets Dauphin 24, 25; goes to
 Poitiers 26; raises siege of
 Orléans 26, 27; wounded 27;
 sees Dauphin crowned 28;
 defeated at Paris 29; taken
 prisoner 29; tried and executed
 30; canonized 31

Laxart, Durand 20, 21
Ligny, Jean de 29
Lisieux, Bishop of 11
Loire, River 4 (map), 20, 22
 (map), 23

Margaret of Antioch, St 16
Maxey 12, 13
Metz, Jean de 21, 22
Meuse, River 4
Michael, Archangel 16, 27

Orléans 22, 26, 27, 31
Oxen 7, 9

Paris 4 (map), 10, 11, 22 (map),
 29, 31
Plague 10, 11
Poitiers 22 (map), 26
Pope 31
Poulengy, Bertrand de 21, 22
Pucelle, La 21

Reims 22, 25, 28
Rouen 10, 22, 30, 31

Saarbruck, Robert de 15
Saints 16
Seine, River 4, 22 (maps)

Taxes 14, 15
Tourelles, Les 27

Vaucouleurs 4 (map), 12, 20, 22,
 31
Vienne, River 22 (map)
Visions 16
Voices 16, 31

Witchcraft 21, 30